Money Management

A Dumbed-Down Version

Take Back Control Of Your Finances, Get Out Of Debt And Become Financially Free

By Adam Richards

Table of Contents

Introduction

What This Book Is About

In the first chapter we will discuss the basics of personal finance, a subject that although every single person has to deal with on an everyday basis, the education system does not have a class about. You will learn why it is so important to start managing your personal finances and the basics of money management and what is expected of you.

In the next chapter, you will learn how to evaluate your current financial situation through a set of 11 questions that will help you determine whether you are financially fit or if now is the time to start making some radical changes.

In the 3rd chapter, we will discuss how you can monitor your income and expenditures and therefore figure out whether or not you are living within your means. You will look at a few essential tools that can be used to make the monitoring process more effective and simple.

In chapter 4, you will learn all about budgeting and how to create one that will fit your needs (and sometimes your wants) according to your own lifestyle. Furthermore, you will find some important tips that can help you make the necessary changes in order to make sure that you are living within your means (and even below) and not going overboard.

In the fifth chapter, we will discuss about bad debt (yeah, there's also good debt btw) and how you can start getting rid of it, if you have already accumulated it. We will go through some tips and strategies that you can implement and will surely help you get rid of your debt without getting even more on top of it.

Finally, in the last chapter you will find a list of 10 effective money habits, that should you start adopting will transform your financial life and help you get back on your feet.

Once again, thank you for purchasing this book, I hope you enjoy it!

Chapter 1:

Personal Finance 101: Things You Didn't Learn At School

We learn many subjects in school ranging from languages and sciences to performing skills like dance and music. However, one skill that is the most needed in our lives is not even introduced to us even in an elementary way. Yes, I am talking about management of personal finances that must be learnt by all. There is no denial in the fact that money rules our life. Unfortunately, very few of us know how to rule money.

During the times of financial abundance or during crises, many individuals lose their financial sanity and often suffer due to the mismanagement of their funds. We all know how to earn but the real test lies on how we spend and manage our financial resources without suffering fiscal hiccups in our day to day lives.

Learning to manage personal finances is not about remembering the rules of budgeting, regulations of accounting or knowing about complicated financial jargon.

It is about knowing how to manage our short-term financial goals, learning to save for future, and creating financial buffers. So, where should you start in order to manage finances effectively and efficiently?

Get Financially Literate

Money is an important aspect of our lives, thus we must learn to manage it effectively. Many financially sound individuals often are at a loss when they have to choose some saving or insurance plan simply because they don't know much about them. They somehow cannot take a judicious and a confident decision even over simple money matters.

While we focus a lot on our communication and vocational skills, it is imperative to pay some attention over learning basic financial skills as well such as:

Banking products and services

Credit cards

Consumer loans

Investments

Insurance

Debt Management

Credit Building

Retirement plans

Income tax management

You might probably overlook the importance of sound money management practices simply because you feel as if you are in control. The truth is, failing to plan on how you are going to use your finances is recipe for failure.

Failure in this case would equate to using money on things that you have not planned for, which means that you might not have money to cater for emergencies when they strike.

Let's take a look at why you need to master how to manage your finances.

Significance of Managing Personal Finances

One of the biggest reasons to embrace money management is that it helps in staying away from bad debts that tend to make our lives extremely miserable. Every individual follows a unique lifestyle and has subjective financial needs. Whatever the conditions, it is very important to follow the waxing and waning of our finances so that our resources can be used optimally. As an old adage says, 'Learn to take care of your money, and it will take care of you', read ahead to find out why proper personal financial management is so crucial:

Pay less interest

When you are in full control of your finances, you don't have to worry about missing credit card payments and payment of various bills or debts, which means that you won't have many instances where you end up paying penalties for late payment. This in turn helps you keep your credit score in check, which means that you can qualify for the best interest rates on mortgage and other loans.

Less stress

Think about it, you really won't need to worry about creditors who keep threatening to report you to the authorities and do many other undesirable acts just to make you to pay any outstanding loans. This means that you can live in greater peace, since you are not under pressure to work; you work because you want to as opposed to working because you have to.

The fact that you don't have any substantial financial security means that you feel vulnerable which amounts to stress.

Greater sense of control

When you master how to manage your finances, you are assured that you can live within your means. You can also allocate your income among the competing financial needs, which include taxes, savings, monthly expenditures and emergencies.

Ease of investing

You can only have the needed peace of mind to invest when you are assured that your financial status is not in a mess. You also won't be scared to invest because you are sure that no one can lay claims on such investments.

#Provide security to your family

You feel in control of your family's future when you have a sound financial management plan that works. This might entail insurance, mortgage and others assets. You can also be assured of maintaining your current living standards even if the unexpected were to happen. This is because of the cushion provided by various investments and assets.

Basics of Money Management

We all need to come to an understanding that money, just like all other economic resources is scarce. In simple terms, you can never have enough of it; even governments don't have enough of it! This means that you must learn the basics so that you can apply them in your day to day life if you are to emerge successful in whatever you do.

In a nutshell, money/financial management at a personal level entails 6 simple points, which you must follow if you are to do anything in life even with limited resources at your disposal:

#1 Personal finance budgeting

#2 Banking

#3 Borrowing and investing and the cost or benefits that come with investing and borrowing

#4 Security of your money

#5 Taxes and their implications

#6 Record or book keeping

After learning what personal financial management entails, you need to go to great lengths just to make sure that everything you do will result to the financial freedom that you probably long for. For you to get to the point of financial freedom thanks to proper personal financial management practices, you need to start somewhere.

Obviously, don't expect to have everything perfect in a day or two; it will take lots of time and deliberate effort to modify your current financial irresponsibility to the desired level of financial control.

To begin this journey, you have to start with knowing where you are so that you can find out where you are going. In any case, how would you know where you are going when you don't know where you are? Makes sense, right?

This means understanding your current financial situation through the evaluation of your income and expenses just to be sure that you are living within your means. Let's discuss this in greater detail in the next chapter.

Chapter 2:

How To Evaluate Your
Current Financial Situation:
Are You Financially Fit?

Now since you have decided to learn about managing your personal finances, let us start by evaluating your current financial situation. To start with, you have to ask yourself several questions just to help you determine whether you are actually living within your means.

Even if it won't show you that you are living beyond your means, you will discover whether you have a money weakness that you need to address if you are to emerge successful in keeping full control of your financial situation.

Answer the following questions:

#1 Do you often lack enough money to cater for your day-to-day expenses?

#2 Do you eat out more often than at home?

#3 Do you desperately wait for your paycheck to manage monthly household expenses? In other words, "Are your living from paycheck to paycheck?"

#4 Do you get lost when someone asks you how much are your household and personal expenses?

#5 Do you get tense when some sudden expense pops up in near or far family circles?

#6 Do you plan your monthly budget?

#7 Do you have any long or short term saving plan?

#8 Can you survive for at least 6 months without your current job or getting any other job? If you cannot survive, you have a problem.

#9 Do your savings account for at least 10% of your income?

#10 Is your mortgage payments less than your one week's income?

#11 Has your credit card balance been reducing over the past year?

If you answered No more than 4 times, you probably have a money problem that you need to address since your income and expenditures are not balanced. In simple terms, you are living beyond your means!

So, what do you do in order to know where the money is going?

To start with, you have to plan on how you are going to monitor your income and expenses if at all you are ever going to control them.

Chapter 3:

Monitoring Income And Expenses: Are You Living Within Your Means?

It is vital to monitor our income and expenses and maintain the right balance otherwise, any disparity will result in debts that would only be mounting and multiplying gradually. For instance, you don't want to get to a point where you hardly have money to pay your bills just because you have spent it on something that isn't really that important.

Therefore, strict monitoring and streamlining of income and expenditure will definitely make it easy for you to start putting control measures so that you can do anything you really want to do with the money. Let's take a look at some practical tips and tricks to help you keep an eye on your income and expenditure.

#Know your expenses closely

Start by understanding each one of your expenditures if you ever want to control the spending. Knowing your expenses will help you know what you are up against based on whether the expenses are necessary or not. Even if you have unexpected costs each month, you MUST ensure that you know them. Keeping a record or list of everything will give you a clear picture of how spendthrift you are.

#Cut the Frivolous expenses

Once you have compiled a comprehensive list of expenses, you can then start analyzing it closely to tell where the money is getting lost due to frivolous purchases. You will be amazed by how easy you will start finding the motivation to cut on unnecessary expenditures when you are aware that you have a money problem.

A while back, I used to like keeping some money in the house because I thought it was more convenient unlike going to the ATM whenever I needed funds. This didn't work out well since I realized that I easily lost track of how much money I was actually spending simply because I would simply pick money without even counting how much was remaining.

I ended up complaining a lot when I realized that my float was always being depleted earlier than I expected; that's when I started keeping track of every expense including buying sweets! Once I knew how much the small unnecessary items were costing me every month, I became very cautious of my spending habits. This meant that I comfortably started saving more just because I could cut on the unnecessary stuff.

#Stop being extravagant

If you have good and steady income, it doesn't mean that all has to be spent even if it means being extravagant. You have to learn how to put aside any surplus so that you can use it when there is a need. This means that you shouldn't spend without a plan and if you expect to have something left to save.

To tame yourself, ensure that you have a budget that includes how much money you must put aside. In any case, you must know the amount of money you spend on necessities and what you spend on unnecessary stuff.

#Develop a habit of wise spending

Wise spending can't be learnt or implemented in a

single day. It is not a procedure, but a habit that has to be developed over time. One can't be a wise spender one particular month and then start misusing their money the next month. It's simple as that.

Once you adopt a habit of proper financial management, you won't have too much stress with respect to being a miser or being a spendthrift. Actually, you should probably enjoy such things like cutting the bills of fast food snacks that tend to have negative effects on your physical and financial wellbeing.

You will in turn start finding satisfaction in such things like fruits and veggies since you know that they are good for you.

Through that, you will have control over your finances and stay healthy in the same time, which means that you will ultimately be saving even more money that would otherwise be spent on treatment caused by unhealthy eating habits.

#Multiply your income

Smart spenders and savers are always on the lookout for chances and avenues that would help them in multiplying their income. If you are a schoolteacher, start taking tuition during your free time. If you are a chef, start giving cooking classes during weekend. The idea is to expand the inflow of money via multiple streams. A small effort from your side will open many avenues for increasing your income.

#Do not carry plenty of cash

Do not carry large amounts of cash or else you will end up spending a lot of it. I know this through experience! Additionally, if you know that you love spending, you might want to leave your debit or credit cards at home. The idea is to create inconvenience for spending.

Therefore, you can follow any viable routine that would prevent you from spending recklessly.

For you to actually monitor your incomes and expenses well, it is best if you have certain tools to help you in your quest towards ensuring that you know everything about your incomes and expenses.

Let's take a look at the essential tools for effective money monitoring.

Calculator

There are specific budgetary calculators that help in keeping track of expenses.

Money Box

Keep a money box handy in your home and use it to store all the receipts and bills that you pay. This will ensure full clarity of all expenditures.

Also, keep in the box a piece of paper that has a record of income.

Diary/ Note-book

Maintain a small pocket diary or a notebook in which you can jot whatever you spend. You would know exactly what have you spent on daily, weekly, fortnightly, or monthly basis.

Mobile phone Apps

With smart phones nowadays, you can download from a variety of applications that can help you in keeping record of your monthly income and expenditures.

After learning how to monitor your expenditures, it is best to understand how you can control it. Budgeting should be your first step towards ensuring that you keep your expenditures in check based on your income. In the next chapter, we will talk about the art of budgeting and how to differentiate between needs and wants if you are to attain financial sanity.

Chapter 4:

Budgeting Explained: How To Create A Budget That Fits Your Needs

Creating a Budget that Fits Our Needs

Budgeting helps in maintaining long term financial health and saves you from living without during unforeseen times of financial crises. Learn to create an effective and a practical budget that would perfectly fit your personal needs. To start with, you need to differentiate between your needs and wants so that you can create the right budget.

Needs Vs Wants

You need to be aware of your needs and wants otherwise you will probably spend money on stuff that is not necessary leaving what is necessary suffering since money is scarce. The things we cannot survive without are our needs such as food, shelter and clothing, etc.

While these are our basic needs for subsistence; we need many more things during different stages of our life.

Wants are the things we can really live without; in simple terms, we won't die if we don't spend on them! Our needs and wants are quite varied.

For instance, you might need a car if you use it actively in your day to day business activities. For someone else on the other hand, a car might not be a necessity according to their current lifestyle and occupation. Likewise, you might need a good computer if your work involves computers, but you really don't need one if you don't do anything that relates to computers (Facebook does not make your computer a necessity either).

Taking a present scenario of life, a family of four can comfortably manage with a 2 bedroom flat and a mid-segment car. This indeed is their need. However, when they start yearning for a large palatial penthouse and a luxury SUV car, they get trapped in the vicious cycle of wants.

The paradox is – Wants never satiate us. Rather, they make us crave even further for bigger homes, latest models of cars and devices, newest brands etc. There is nothing wrong about that by the way. As human beings we tend to always crave for more, BUT not if those wants end up crippling our financial future.

You have to differentiate between your needs and wants before you can even start budgeting. You need to be honest with yourself and be objective about determining whether you actually need something or you simply want it.

By differentiating between your needs and wants, you can be sure that whatever expenditure items you allocate funds for will really be necessary.

So, how do you prepare a budget that meets your needs and not wants?

#Simplify your budget

A practical budget is the one that is simple to make, understand as well as apply. Any kind of financial jargon is a complete no-no to be included in a budget. Make it realistic and close to your habits and tendencies so that you can stick to it consistently.

#Consistent time span

Don't just prepare short term budgets since this might easily make you lose track of your long-term goals. As you budget, ensure that the budget period is consistent since this will help you in nurturing proper spending habits.

A reasonable time span to test a budget should be at least one year. This would include all sorts of inflow and outflow of money including taxes and vacation expenses. This doesn't mean that you shouldn't budget for each day, week or month!

#Ensure that you have funds for emergencies

While preparing your budget, take into consideration contingency funds so that unforeseen expenses can be taken care of. This fund will also cater for such things like medical emergencies. Through that, you will be sure that you won't suffer substantial financial problems even with minor emergencies.

In simple terms, your life shouldn't stop simply because you have to pay DUI charges!

#A comprehensive budget

A good budget would be the one that would take care of the entire family and their needs collectively. Do not forget any family member starting from young kids and their baby-sitting expenditures to elderly grandparents and their medical bills.

#Be flexible

Don't consider your budget to be a prophetic piece of work. It is good to stick to your budget but be flexible to make some changes to get everything running smoothly.

It is always better to make some minor to major changes in the budget rather than waiting for it to fail.

#Increase your income

If your budget is making you live frugally but hurting your temperament, look for ways of pumping in more money in the budget kitty. This way, you can have less of cost cutting and enjoy your life comfortably.

#Watch your mindset

You shouldn't start feeling bad because of your budget otherwise you will soon stop implementing it. Instead, you should approach the issue with an open mind so that you can derive the most from your budgeting efforts.

The entire budgeting process can be summarized into 6 simple steps, which you have to follow religiously if you are to break free from improper spending habits.

Budgeting Made Simple – 6 Steps

Step #1

Understand your financial and personal situation so you can assess your values, needs and current situation in life, so that you can come up with a **SMART** budget. A smart budget will be specific, measurable, attainable, realistic and time bound.

Step #2

Set your financial and personal goals. These should be closely linked to ensure that you work towards blending budgeting with your lifestyle.

Step #3

Set a budget for all variable expenses and fixed expenses depending on how much money you make within a certain period. In this budget, ensure you include everything that needs money. While preparing the budget, ensure that you don't have thoughts about any more money you might get from elsewhere; otherwise you might be tempted to increase your expenses.

Step #4

Monitor your current spending (investing and saving) patterns and do something about it. Your budget should already have an allocation for savings and investments.

Step #5

Compare the budget to what you actually spent during the specific budget period. This means that you must keep records of everything you spend on.

Step #6

Review your progress and make the necessary budgetary changes.

I know that this seems quite simple to implement. However, a lot goes into ensuring that you actually spend only what you have budgeted for. This can be especially difficult if you don't have a habit of using money appropriately.

To solve this problem, it is paramount that you start adopting a lifestyle of living within your means. I know that budgeting is all about enabling you to live within your means. However, it is worth talking about how you can actually develop a culture or habit of living this lifestyle.

Mastering How To Live Within And Even Below Your Means

Money needs a wise mind and steady hands for its judicious use. The idea of earning and saving money is to lead a comfortable life where nothing is wasted or unaccounted for. Money should not be spent to impress the world, as this is a purely illogical interpretation of happiness.

Let's take a look at some important tips you can use to start living within your means as opposed to dancing to every tune of buying this and that just to meet your consumerism desires.

Understanding the concept of wealth

Different people nurture different perceptions of being rich and wealthy.

While some consider having a palatial house and a luxury car a symbol of being rich, others consider having enough for their family's wants, needs with some sensible and regular saving.

Although there is nothing wrong in being ambitious to earn all sorts of luxuries (if you are reading this book, you do have the potential to do that), living a life on credit or in bad debts should be the last thing to consider.

Share and Save

There are many ways to save money in a smarter and intelligent way. One category of people drive to work daily alone in their car while others take the train or bus despite the fact they can very well afford a car. Some even form a carpool where colleagues take out their cars in turns while others commute together. Of course, the second category is smarter in its thinking and has higher chances on staying financially stress-free.

Be a Smart and Not an Impulsive Shopper

Wise spenders have great control of their finances and don't spend impulsively. Instead, they buy what they need and ensure that they get the most value for their money.

Don't go to the mall for window shopping

When you need something, go to a proper retail store that is offering quality goods on discounted prices.

Shun advertisements

Do not believe advertisements as they are devised in such a way as to make you believe you cannot live without that product. There is nothing wrong about that, that's their job and they are darn good at it. However, you should minimize your exposure to ads and TV if you really want to keep your desire to buy at bay.

Compare and Buy

Comparison of price may need some time and effort but will certainly save you money. Comparing the price of things and services will actually allow you to save even more. You can look out for companies that list price discounts in different stores just to be sure that you are getting the best deal.

Have the bigger picture in mind

Don't think about saving your money for short term. All your plans should somehow help you to live a good life when you get to a point when you cannot work.

Learn to stay frugal

By staying frugal, you will be helping no one else but yourself. We all know that we will never have enough of what we see advertised on TV and all over the internet; that's what consumerism is all about!

Buy what you need and can afford easily. Want more? Then earn more but still spend wisely and stay within your means.

Be Safe and Healthy

Being sick or being involved in an accident can cause havoc to your finances. Stay healthy and safe can prevent draining your savings.

Rather, invest in your fitness so that you can enjoy not just your money but also a healthy and vibrant life.

Curb Extravaganza

Are your friends going out for dinner? Think twice before joining them. Are you going because you haven't been out with them for a long time or just for the sake of it?

Learn to entertain yourself at home as opposed to going out since if you go out, you will probably spend more money than you expected.

Manage Time to Manage Money

Many times, we have to pay penalty on bills and invoices for exceeding the last date of payment. Learn to monitor when different bills are due to ensure that you don't end up missing your payments.

You may automate the process just to ensure that everything is under control.

Chapter 5:

How To Get Rid Of Bad Debt And Become Financially Healthy

Debts are one of the most annoying things that can easily affect our need to manage our personal finances. However, debts are not always bad. Interestingly, some of them are good.

Good debt is not a liability; actually, it's an investment that tends to make our money grow over a longer period, giving us the opportunity to make optimal use of liquid cash. One appropriate example of good debt is education loan that is taken to pay for college or higher education.

Taking an education loan doesn't always mean that the borrower cannot afford paying the fee in cash. This loan is also taken in order to take advantage of low interest rate of education loan. If you are a student, you don't have to burden your parents with the fees and can have your fees catered for by the student loan. You can then start repaying your education loan when you have completed your education and have started earning a salary.

Mortgage is also considered a good debt as it is considered to be a money saver in the longer run. So, basically a good debt enables you to benefit in one way or another in the future.

In contrast to good debts, bad debts are taken to buy those things or services that lose their worth fast and do not create any promising income in the long term. I mean that if you borrow money and once you repay the loan, you do not derive any benefit from what you used the borrowed funds to undertake, then that was bad debt.

Bad debts also come accompanied with a higher rate of interest. One common example of bad debt is credit card debt, which is known for creating a vicious circle of financial liabilities. Buying flashy and branded luxuries through your credit card and then feeling helpless over its non-payment for years to come is a classic example of bad debt.

Other types of bad debts are cash advance loans and payday loans that charge astronomical rates of interest that get compounded if not paid on time. These kinds of loans are devised to take advantage of your pathetic and helpless financial condition.

Getting Rid of Bad Debt

Now that you know bad debt is not good for you, how do you get rid of it? Just like a debt can't be accumulated in a single day, it can't be resolved on a single day. The primary requisite to manage our personal finances is to keep away from debts.

If you already have a few of them, start planning strategically so as to get rid of them as soon as possible. We will look at some effective tips and strategies to help you get rid of those bad debts.

Document all your debt

It is imperative that you identify and document all your debt. I mean how you can plan to get rid of bad debts when you don't even know how much debt you owe to your friends, credit card companies and the bank. You can use a spreadsheet to record all the debt that you own to different people. Once you do this, decide on the bad debts that you would want to get rid of first.

I would suggest that you start with the debt with the smallest amount, as you will be more motivated and once you have cleared it you will see that you are actually getting rid of debts rather than paying one large debt that never seems to end. By the time you get to the large amounts, you would be motivated enough to keep going.

Do not add more debts

If you are already debt ridden, just stop there. Do not add more to your already loaded financial burdens. You ought to concentrate on resolving past financial liabilities, and not accumulating more.

Ignore your credit cards

Credit cards are the biggest reason and cause of bad debts. This financial product gives ready cash to spenders and makes them reckless and mindless consumers. Just keep them away and learn to live without them.

Using a credit card simply makes for uncontrolled spending that leads to further financial mess. Do not close your credit card accounts until all debts against them are repaid back, if you don't want to have your credit score affected.

Identify all of your liquid assets.

Liquid assets are simply items that can be easily turned to cash. This however does not mean that you pawn your wife's engagement ring. The goal is to find those things that you don't use; sell them and get some money to reduce your debt. Don't make the mistake of selling those items only to use the money on unnecessary expenditures as this will defeat the whole purpose.

Develop a sensible attitude

Debt accumulation does not happen out of need but out of lax attitude towards money. This calls for immediate change in attitude so that whatever causes debt can be cured. A strong will to develop a frugal and judicious attitude towards money, will certainly take care of many financial issues that are known to be caused due to an irresponsible mindset.

Most people usually have the tendency to think that debt or a loan is free money without understanding that you will surely need to pay that money in the future. When you adopt the attitude that money borrowed is not actually your money, you will be more careful with debt management.

Alter your spending tendencies

Are you a mindless spender who buys not out of need but out of greed? If you are such a person who cannot restrain buying things that are not even needed, you need to deal with this problem. You need to figure out where your need to spend stems from. In most cases, people who love spending a lot sort of derive love and satisfaction from the things they buy. You should better find a new way of being happy and joyful other than spending money on different items.

I would suggest that before you buy anything; give it some days or even a week to sink in. If you still remember that you need something after the week has passed, then go ahead and make the purchase. However, in most cases you will notice that you will not even remember if you needed something the previous day.

Follow a thrifty lifestyle

Since we live in the era of consumerism, we have started believing that there are many things that are simply indispensable for our subsistence. This is a wrong approach as we are the ones who are responsible for expanding our wants, mistaking them for needs. To ensure that we are debt free, following a thrifty lifestyle is the way to go.

Increase your income

While cost cutting is always suggested for getting rid of debts, opening multiple income channels will speed up the process. Increasing your income will make the journey towards getting rid of debt much easier.

Moreover, earning extra is never going to hurt you anyway. Income can be increased by doing any such thing that interests you.

It could be either some money-making hobby like teaching, cooking, music, dance, or aerobics or some skill like being a singer, writer, or carpenter etc. Having an alternative income channel will cushion your financial crises.

Avoid penalties and overcharges

Understand that you are already in debt and paying extra and extra charges that can be certainly avoided will drain your resources.

Do not delay paying bills, do not jump traffic rules, do not drive while drunk as these are some of the cases where you may have to use a lot of money and it would be out of sheer negligence and carelessness.

Some other ways to save precious extra dollars (or whatever currency you use for that matter) are:

\# Going to bank for withdrawing money instead of ATM

\# Avoiding online booking of tickets

\# Negotiating rates of interest on your credit card

\# Consolidating your multiple loans into one single loan that has a lower interest rate.

Most of all, have a budget

There is a high likelihood that you are where you right now, cause of your inability to budget your expenditures. It is crucial that you know how you spend money on different items so that you can know what you spend most money on and make the necessary plans to streamline your expenditure. Furthermore, when you are aware of how you are spending your money, you are less likely to overspend.

Chapter 6:

Stick To It: 10 Powerful Money Habits That Can Transform Your Financial Life

Now let's see ten incredibly powerful habits that should incorporated can dramatically transform your finances and by extend your life.

#1 Develop acumen to differentiate between need and wants. This will help in having clear financial objectives pertaining to long term as well as short term.

#2 Remain financially aware and get educated so that no one can take you for a ride. You should have a habit of checking and cross checking your bank details, interest rates, and credit reports. Don't be alien to these important things.

#3 Learn to pay close attention to menial yet important details such as your grocery bills, the rates of day to day utilities, and discounted schemes on offers etc.

#4 Get into the habit of thinking innovatively to save your money. It could be like using solar power that would reduce power bills. You can start accumulating shopping points and rewards to redeem them later and get some real great stuff.

The idea is to develop a habit of saving by being proactive, aware and intelligent.

#5 Do not be lazy lest you find that you spend a lot of money on unnecessary things. For instance, instead of eating out or ordering take-out, why not cook. Instead of taking a cab, why not use the bus or the train.

While these small things may not seem as much, when you compile the total money you can save, you will be amazed.

#6 Always look for quality and not price. This is a proven fact that quality things are reliable and do not require frequent maintenance that call for a lot of overheads.

Buying a cheap pair of shoes over quality (not necessarily branded) shoes is always going to be an unworthy deal as the shoes will soon wear out and you would have to buy another pair soon.

This habit finds great relevance especially in buying household utilities and fixtures. In short, the cheaper option may not always be a cost-viable option.

#7 Be a year-round negotiator. Always ask for a discount on every purchase you make. Don't be embarrassed in doing so, as the worst the suppler can say is just no.

If you are more interested in developing your negotiation skills, you can check out my book *"Negotiation: How To Nurture Your Negotiation Skills, Overcome Any Objections In Life And Get The Best Possible Deal Always"*.

#8 Develop the habit of saving. You should try as much as possible to save at least 10% of your income. Saving can be a real help in accruing your funds and then investing them to earn even more income.

Find a good and an effective saving method (saving accounts or fixed deposits) and start keeping some amount consistently without fail.

 # 9 Question insurance premium renewals. I know we are all guilty of simply paying an insurance premium renewal without first knowing if the charges are still the same, the changes made in the insurance premium as well as if it is the best deal.

Each year, before you renew your insurance premium, call at least another insurance company to know if you are getting the best deal. I mean, there is so much that can happen within a year.

#10 Last but not the least, replacing your credit card with your debit card is one habit that needs to be adopted soon. This is critical, as it will ensure that you are not a victim of impulse buying.

Rather, it is suggested to stop keeping your credit card in your wallet. It should only be used for maintaining your credit record.

Conclusion

Personal finance is one of the most underrated subjects, yet in my opinion the most important one. We deal with money on a daily basis, so you would think that it would be common sense to learn more about it, right?

How many people you know that have actually read a book or two on money management? Not many, right?

Therefore, congratulations are in order. No only you decided to pick up this book because you want to learn more about effective money management (that speaks volumes btw), you actually went through and read it.

Now is the time to put to good use the tips and strategies that you have learned so far and take massive action. It will not be long until you see your first results and trust me, when that happens you will more motivated than ever to keep calm and carry on.

I will be more than happy to learn how this book has helped you in some way. If you feel you have learned something or you think it offered you some value, please take a moment to leave an honest review on Amazon. It would help many future readers who will be forever grateful to you. As I will!

To Your Success,
Adam Richards

DISCLAIMER AND/OR LEGAL NOTICES:

Every effort has been made to accurately represent this book and it's potential. Results vary with every individual, and your results may or may not be different from those depicted. No promises, guarantees or warranties, whether stated or implied, have been made that you will produce any specific result from this book. Your efforts are individual and unique, and may vary from those shown. Your success depends on your efforts, background and motivation.

The material in this publication is provided for educational and informational purposes. Use of the programs, advice, and information contained in this book is at the sole choice and risk of the reader.